1 In 1900 a day by the river in Richmond was a treat. The pace of life was reflected in the elegant ease of strolling on the towpath

2 *(overleaf)* Guildford High Street with the old guildhall on the left. The clock hanging outside it was hung in 1683, but the works date back to 1560

Victorian and Edwardian

SURREY

from old photographs

Introduction and commentaries by

MARTYN GOFF

B. T. BATSFORD LTD
LONDON

for Rubio Tapani Lindroos

B. T. Batsford Ltd
4, Fitzhardinge St, London W.1
Printed and bound in Great Britain by
Anchor Brendon Ltd, Tiptree, Essex
First published in 1972
Reprinted 1974, 1984

ISBN 0 7134 0123 0

3 Coach and horses outside the White Horse Hotel, Dorking. Some parts of
this building are more than 400 years old

CONTENTS

ACKNOWLEDGMENTS

Books like this one are built very largely on the help of others. We are indebted for the photographs to: Banstead District Library (73); W. J. Brunell (58); R. G. Burr and Surrey County Library (157); M. Bushley (49, 57, 60, 97, 112); Caterham & Warlingham District Library (123); Croydon Public Library (48, 53, 61, 68, 87, 90, 91, 93, 95, 96, 98–100, 108, 113, 118, 126, 130, 131, 133, 138, 140, 152, 159, 160); William Gordon Davis (1, 5); Esher District Library (31, 51, 122, 132, 134, 150); Lord Freyberg for all the late Gertrude Jekyll's photographs (75, 79–86, 94); F. Frith & Co. Ltd. (29, 33, 34, 65, 71, 105, 109, 116, 120, 165, 167); Horley District Library (149); Mrs Hylton-Foster (76, 77, 129, 143); Kingston-on-Thames District Library (74, 92); London Transport Executive (14, 20); Mansell Collection (*frontispiece,* 23, 142); Minet Collection [Olney Collection] (50); Minet Library (6–13, 15, 28, 36–47, 119, 139); National Rifle Association (144–46); Radio Times Hulton Picture Library (18, 22, 30); Richmond Public Library (16, 19, 21, 25, 27, 59, 148, 151); Surrey County Cricket Club (137); J. Valentine (107); Weybridge Museum (54–56, 78, 89, 161, 162); Thomas A. Wilkie (101–103, 156, 159). The remainder of the photographs are from the Publisher's collection.

I would particularly like to thank Miss Williams of the Minet Library, Lambeth; Mr J. F. Viles of the Banstead Public Library; Miss Molly Liggett, the Guildford Chief Librarian; Mr L. C. Silverthorne, the Caterham Librarian; and Miss M. Gollancz, the Surrey County Archivist, for help and advice. Nor would the book have been achieved without the assistance of Mrs Marjory Vernon, Mrs Emily Taylor, Mr Rubio Tapani Lindroos and Miss Jane Morris, my ever helpful secretary.

INTRODUCTION

Scale is the dominant impression after looking through hundreds of Victorian and Edwardian photographs: Man was still in control of the creations. There were no Centrepoints nor Vickers Towers: no Post Office Towers nor Hiltons. If this was true of London and other cities, it was even more so of semi-rural counties like Surrey. It was only semirural because the Surrey of those days included much that is now London: Wimbledon, Lambeth, Putney, Southwark, Dulwich. Surrey, shorn of its Thameside districts, is still a vertical county. Buildings like the Tolworth Tower (the ubiquitous Colonel Seifert) are rare enough to emphasise rather than deny this.

Surrey is, too, a county of vanished palaces. Oatlands and Nonsuch and the Archiepiscopal Palace at Croydon have all gone. It is hard to believe that:

> The Palace of Oatlands was a structure of great extent and complexity. The foundations are said to have been traced over an area of 14 acres. . . . It was built of red brick, with stone quoins and dressings, gables, bays, and ornamental chimney shafts, somewhat after the fashion of Hampton Court.

Elizabeth I often stayed at Oatlands early in her reign; so did James I in his. After Charles I it was razed to the ground, but in 1725 the Earl of Lincoln built a new house in its place. This in its turn was enlarged and remodelled by his grandson, the Duke of Newcastle, so that Horace Walpole had first thought of it as 'the centre of Paradise', though later felt it 'not half so Elysian as I used to think'. Magic must have been in the air, not least because of its fabled shell-work Grotto (still there!); but by 1858 it had become the Oatlands Park Hotel, and soon after, much of its famous park was 'built over with first class villas'.

But palaces, past and present, are but icing. Underneath, the cake is solid, and above all, respectable. There were colliers and tramps and gipsies and much poverty in late Victorian Surrey, but there was also great wealth. The villas of Streatham and Tooting and Clapham, however unlikely it may sound now, were the homes of the new merchants, dignified, correct, Church-going, utterly conformist. Farther out, in what is still Surrey, were the landed gentry and the very rich. As near to London as Richmond, a list of some of the more important houses and their owners in 1875 tells us a great deal:

Wick House, then belonging to A. Tod, Esq (originally built for Sir Joshua Reynolds)
Ancaster House: Lieut.-Col. F. Burdett
Lansdowne House: The Marquis of Lansdowne
Cardigan House: J. Willis Esq (formerly the house of the Earl of Cardigan)
Downe House: Hon. Mrs Broadhurst (once Sheridan's house)
Queensbury House: Thos. Cave Esq MP

Buccleuch House: The Duke of Buccleuch
Camborne House: The Duchess-Dowager of Northumberland

Richmond's population at this time was just under 20,000 people. All Surrey, as then constituted, numbered 1,433,899, but nearly a million of these lived in what is now Greater London. There was clearly room for so many large houses with their extensive grounds. Guildford, on the River Wey, had about half of Richmond's population in the 1880's; Kingston about the same as its nearby town. Even in a county only 25 miles from north to south and 39 from east to west there was plenty of room: once again the scale was right.

Guildford and Kingston were the chief towns outside the Metropolitan area, with the Spring Assizes at Kingston and the Summer at Guildford. Both had markets several days a week. It is a cautionary thought that the total police force numbered only 150 men, 20 sergeants and 13 officers, not forgetting a chief constable: work must have been light; traffic certainly was. There were also two military depots, one in each of the two chief towns.

The industrial revolution seems hardly to have brushed against Surrey. A contemporary register proudly claims market gardening, brush broom and paper making, and potteries. Godalming surprisingly had hosiery and woollen goods. Nutfield and Reigate were centres for the digging of Fuller's earth from which woollen fabrics were made. The former factory, eerie and beautiful at night, can still be seen right against the main London–Brighton road just south of Redhill.

Even in this day of ecological warnings it seems almost impossible to believe that the 11-mile-long River Wandle, rising in Croydon and entering the Thames at Wandsworth, was 'one of the best trout streams in the south of England'. Both nearly four times as long as the Wandle, the Wey and the Mole could really be described as the chief rivers of Surrey, much of the former being navigable. But of course in Victorian times the Thames was Surrey's chief river; and we still, at Boat Race time, talk of the 'Surrey Bank' as the two boats go skimming up the river.

Much of Surrey's rapid emergence as a commuters' area was due to the early excellence of its railway services. By 1841 there was already a line from London to Croydon in existence. By the end of the century there was the London, Brighton & South Coast Railway from London to Brighton via Croydon, Red Hill (*sic*) and Horley; to Eastbourne via Oxted; and to Portsmouth via Dorking and Epsom. The London and South-Western Railway had lines to Woking, Esher and Guildford. And the South-Eastern Railway went to Tonbridge and Reading via Croydon and Redhill. Reigate's refusal, in fact, to have the main Brighton line directly caused the rapid growth of Redhill which had gladly accepted it.

Human scale, respectability, a good sprinkling of landed gentry and a reasonable railway service drew the professionals and merchants in ever-increasing numbers as the century came to its end, but there was another quality: Surrey is a beautiful county.

Box Hill might be ten miles away; Leith Hill or Hindhead never visited. Yet these three, and 50 others less dramatic, are what has always given the right ring to living in Surrey. 'I live in Surrey' conjures up immediately the marvellous line of the North Downs, the Hog's Back with its stunning views, the Old Way (often called the Pilgrims' Way, running along the southern side of the North Downs), Guildford's High Street and Farnham's Castle. The list is long.

There was, though, an indigenous population. Perrots Manor, at Banstead, was bought by John Lambert from the Charlwoods in 1515. In the Garratt's chapel of Banstead's All Saints Church a stone reads: 'Thomas Lambert, gent, sometime yeoman of the chamber to King James and King Charles.' Close to it is a memorial to Sir Daniel Lambert MP, who died in 1745. The Lamberts remained one of the squires of the neighbourhood throughout the Victorian era; and some of them are still there.

At the other end of the scale there were farmers and labourers and carters and bricklayers who rarely ventured more than ten miles from their birthplaces throughout their lives. Gertrude Jekyll, in her fascinating *Old West Surrey* (Longmans, Green 1904, reprinted 1971 by S. R. Publishers), gives some wonderful verbal and photographic portraits of these people. She provides a splendid picture, for example, of the rough but effective group morality of Surrey folk in Victorian times:

> If a man was known to beat his wife, he was first warned. The warning was a quiet enough one – not a word was spoken; but some one went at night with a bag of chaff, and laid a train of it from the roadway up to the cottage door. It meant, 'We know that thrashing is going on here.' If the man took the hint and treated his wife better, nothing more happened. But if the ill-treatment went on, a number of men and boys came some other night with kettles and pans and fire-irons, and anything they could lay their hands on to make a noise with, and give him 'Rough Music'. The din was something dreadful, but the effect was said to be salutary. My home was half a mile from the village, but every now and then on summer nights we used to hear the discordant strains of this orchestra of public protest and indignation.

Miss Jekyll also has some fascinating figures about the earnings of these local folk. Farm labourers' were paid between 13/- and 16/- (65–80p) a week, though the rent of their cottages was only 2/- (10p) a week. Hours, too, were incredibly long. A Godalming carpenter finished a fencing job in Portsmouth one evening at 5.30, then walked all night the 37 miles back home to be ready at his master's place at 6 next morning for the day's instructions!

Surrey has no real dialect of its own. Local words are nearly all common to Kent and Sussex. In this connection it is worth remembering that the very border between Kent and Surrey was disputed as late as the seventeenth century. A solemn inquiry conducted by judges then found Hatcham to be in Surrey. It has few major events in English history, and hardly any wars. Magna Carta was signed just within its boundaries; and there was a Civil War battle somewhere between Kingston and Nonsuch Palace. On the latter occasion the Royalists were defeated and driven across the Thames. Its cohesion as a county comes from scenery and, to a lesser extent, people. And in Victorian times that cohesion did not really exist: it was half country, half metropolis.

Surrey gains its reputation from its scenery – and from its townscapes. Guildford High Street, Compton, Abinger Hammer, Lingfield, Dorking High Street: the list could cover many lines. Nearly every town and village has a church of some merit; and a few old houses or other buildings. But they are being swamped. The first reaction to the photographs that follow is one of pleasant interest: 'how quaint it all was! Is that what Dorking High Street looked like at the end of the last century?' But a second and third look replace the pleasure with alarm, if not horror. How far have we already destroyed the beautiful buildings and glorious scenery that made Victorian Surrey so desirable a place to live in or visit! This is no sentimental plea of a back to ye olde tea shoppe nature; but an alert to a movement that can only wipe out everything but efficiency, speed and the media – cars, concrete, computers – to achieve them.

Let us enjoy these pictures of Victorian and Edwardian Surrey, even to laughing at our forebears' pretentions and taste. But let us also remember that, on the whole, Surrey has deteriorated since these pictures were taken. It just might persuade us to call a halt.

Martyn Goff

4   Administration of the Granville Charity in the Churchyard of Wotton on February 2nd 1872. John Evelyn, the great diarist is buried here, as is his wife

ALONG THE RIVER

5   Richmond: taking a boat out on the water (1900)

6   Lambeth Palace (c. 1860), which takes its name from 'loam-hythe' or muddy harbour, in the days before the busy surrounding streets were cleared away

7   Bishop's Walk, Lambeth (c. 1860) with the Palace wall on the left. Now the site of St Thomas's Hospital that is itself being rebuilt

8 Lambeth Palace and the Bishop's Walk before the Albert Embankment was built. This 1860 photograph ante-dates the change by 20 years

9 Wandsworth High Street, 1898, now, alas, all changed and being submerged by the vast Arndale Centre. The district's name, originally Wandlesworth, celebrates its being north of the confluence of the Thames and the Wandle

10 *Feathers Boat Inn*, Wandsworth, at the mouth of the Wandle River that meanders away through Tooting and Wimbledon and Wallington to a lake in Croydon

11   Putney Bridge, first opened in 1729, was flooded in 1881. Five years later the future King Edward VII opened the new five-arch bridge

12   Toll House Keeper, Putney Bridge, 1880. By 1731 £1500 a year was being collected in tolls, and this had doubled by the end of the century

13   Putney High Street, 1879. None of the buildings remain; and the present nondescript street, almost always jammed with traffic, seems narrower than its predecessor

14   Putney High Street from Putney Bridge. All the buildings on the right are still there, including the *White Lion Hotel* itself. The replacements for those on the left, long since demolished, are themselves coming down already!

15 Putney: the freezing of the Thames outside the *Eight Bells* pub in 1887 (shades of Virginia Woolf's *Orlando*)

16 Upper Richmond Road–Roehampton Lane crossroads. The thatched cottage, neatly spruced up, is still there. *The Railway Hotel*, in a variety of colours, has become *The Red Rover*

17 *The Bull Hotel*, and its neighbour *The Waterman's Arms*, still proudly front the river, though the trees beyond have given way to a hideous Police Station that looks like a public convenience.

18 Kew Gardens in 1864, just over a hundred years after it was founded by Princess Augusta

19 Old Kew Bridge (around 1895). The seven-arch structure was designed by James Paine and built between 1783 and 1789 by Robert Tunstall. Later it was bought for £22,000 by a Mr G. Robinson and finally, in 1873, by the Government for £57,300, when it was freed from toll

20 Kew Green. The inn sign and the green are still intact. Continuous traffic flow have banished for ever the peaceful rural look

21 Old Kew Bridge being demolished in 1899

22 Richmond Bridge in 1880, one hundred and three years after it was first opened. Designed by Paine and Couse, it cost £26,000

23 (*overleaf*) Bend in the river just below Richmond Hill: the boat-house remains, though tightly wedged between a brace of buildings. But gone are the elegant ladies and their parasols from the opposite towpath

24   The Terrace at Richmond is wonderfully unspoilt, but the nannies have long since gone; and their charges are far more likely to be wearing denim shorts or tiny bikinis

25   Lower George Street, Richmond, now nearly engulfed by the busy one-way system. The building on the left, the tiny shop in the centre and the one next to it on its right remain. But – oh! – the horses' drinking trough has become – A Gentlemen's Lavatory!

26   High Street, Kingston-upon-Thames, c. 1896. The market and assize town's population was only just over 27,000 people at that time. Anglo-Saxon kings were crowned in Kingston: thus its name

27   The Market Place, Kingston-upon-Thames, 1892, with the old town hall in the background on the left. This Italianate building, designed by Henman, was erected in 1840. The statue on the front balustrade is of Queen Anne

28 Kingston Toll Bridge, 1869. It was opened in 1828 by the Queen Dowager Adelaide and freed from tolls a year after this photograph was taken

29 Kingston Bridge, 1890, with Bond's Family Hotel next to it. The bridge was designed by Lapidge and has five large span arches and two smaller flanking ones

30 Queen's Road, Surbiton, a very grand address in 1896. Visually little changed from across the river, the large villas are now all divided into flats and bedsits

31 Hampton Court Club and Tagg's Boat House on a club regatta day, now alas, a launch-building factory

32   Molesey Lock, with boats coming over the rollers, 1896, is near the confluence of the Mole and the Thames

33 Church Street, Walton-on-Thames, 1903. Tradition has it that Charles I's death warrant was signed in *The House of President Bradshaw* in this street

34 Bridge Street, Walton-on-Thames, 1903

SURREY IN LONDON

35   The Falcon Tavern, Clapham Junction, 1863. The population of Clapham
about this time was only just over 25,000!

36 *The Plough Inn* at Clapham. Trams, complete with adverts on their sides, were to go on until 1950, though not with horses!

37 Middle-class Bedford Hill at Balham, now many rungs down the scale

38 Newington Butts, so called by reason of its archery and to distinguish it from Newington in North London

39 Streatham Common, looking very rural still at the turn of the century

40 *The Greyhound*, Streatham, 1860. There's still an inn by that name, but completely without the rural charm or appearance

41 Old Farm, Greyhound Lane, Streatham. As late as 1875 the population was still less than 12,000. The new merchant rich had their splendid villas in what a century earlier had been a well-known spa

42 Dulwich College, originally founded in 1619 by Edward Alleyne, entirely rebuilt in 1868 by Charles Barry, son of the greater architect of the same name

43 Dulwich Park: *The sylvan wilds*
     Of Dulwich yet by barbarous arts unspoiled

44   Westow Hill, Upper Norwood, with one of the Crystal Palace towers in the centre background

45   The Crystal Palace, originally transferred from the 1851 Festival at Hyde Park, became a great show place. At a concert there early in this century, a whisper during a pianissimo passage for the strings was heard right across the vast hall: "I always fry mine in oil."

47   Hill Road, Wimbledon, at a point where, horses, carts and people apart, it doesn't look so different now

48   A saw-pit on Wimbledon Common, c. 1888. Always placed on top of hills so that they would keep dry by natural draining, 'top-sawyer' came to mean someone rather grand

46   (*overleaf*) Boys picking bluebells on Wimbledon Common, with short hair tucked under (usually felt) caps

TRANSPORT

49 William Bashford, who was born and lived in Outwood

50 A Cycling Club in the 1880's in the Upper Richmond Road. The gear would not look out of place in the contemporary King's Road, Chelsea

51 A group of early AA patrols outside the *Hut Hotel*, Wisley. In those days they would even warn the motorist of imminent speed traps

52   Off to, or arriving at, some splendid occasion, splendidly got up

53   An omnibus in the Upper Richmond Road around 1895 (then known as The Parade). Thomas Tilling still exist, but as a conglomorate owning companies producing everything from ladies stockings to books, rather than as a bus company

54 Brooklands Motor Track, Weybridge, in the year it was built, 1907. It was built by Hugh Locke King on his own land for testing cars at the time of the 4 m.p.h. limit (plus a man in front with a red flag!). And in the original races, the drivers wore their own colours, like jockeys, and called the starting point 'the paddock'

55 The airfield was in the middle of the Brooklands Race Track, though no flying was allowed during a car race

56 Not only was the flying field in the middle of the Brooklands Race Track, but so were the sewage works in 1910!

57 H.M.A. *Delta* at Earlswood, July 2nd 1913

58 The Ewell watersplash on the way to the Derby early in the century. The Daimler probably stayed some hours; the coach and horse hurried on

59 Richmond Station, 1889. Those were the days – apparently – when porters outnumbered passengers

60 Reigate, November 1896: the first motor car almost totally surrounded by carriages and people

SURREY VILLAGES

61 The Post Office at Sanderstead, 1896. This pretty, secluded village, nearly 600 feet up on the North Downs, then had a population of 267 souls!

62 Cobham: Leigh Hill, 1903

63 Woodcote Green, part of Epsom, where the Baltimore family once had a great house. 'Let us come', wrote Martin Tupper, 'to Ebba's Ham, the notorious Epsom, famed alike for purgatives and races'

64 Ruxley Watersplash, Epsom

65   Shere Village, still one of the prettiest villages in England, and dated here only by the children's clothes

66 Quaint cottages, a winding street, a great house and a church give so many villages an incomparable air of calm, history and Englishness. This is true of Betchworth, where three of the Church's lancet windows are 700 years old

67 Thursley Village, with its Saxon church and two charming old houses, little changed to this day

68 The main street of Oxted, 1890. The older part of Oxted still preserves some of the quintessential charm in this picture

69 Carshalton Pond. It is still there, relatively unspoiled (and with the base much improved). But children no longer paddle, nor horses wade across. . . .

70 The Anchor Hotel, Ripley, was new when Elizabeth I rode through the village

71 Pyrford Mill in 1903, near the ruins of the great Newark Priory, a striking building of white boards and red roofs

72   The Victoria, Banstead High Street. Still there, and not too much changed, though the pond just glimpsed on the right is now filled in and crowned with an ugly parade of shops

73   The Old Well, Banstead, c. 1909. It's still there, though the Lodge to Yewlands just behind it has become a row of nondescript houses, while Rosehill (formerly Rooks Nest), the grand house on the right down Park Road, is a property developer's offices

74 High Street, Church Cobham, 1906. This part of Cobham, built around the Church of St Andrew, is on the right bank of the River Mole, with Cobham Street half a mile away on the main Portsmouth Road

RURAL SURREY

75 Well-winch, used particularly on higher ground where the water lay at deeper levels

76 A summer garden scene at Tolworth (at that time Talworth) in 1885, long before Richard Seifert's great tower dominated the former hamlet. Walword, writing that same year in *Greater London* (Cassell's 2 vols.) complained that the 'town is still struggling with country. Long lines of villas stretch in every direction, and are gradually overcoming the rural character of the district.'

77 A group at the Tolworth tennis club grounds in 1885

78 (*overleaf*) The staff at Claremont, the home earlier in the century of Prince Leopold, later first King of the Belgians. The future Queen Victoria often stayed there and spent the first ten birthdays of her reign in the house. Louis Philippe lived and died there after the revolution of 1848. Capability Brown designed the house and grounds for Clive of India. It is now a fine girls' school

79 Countrywoman, early twentieth century. These were simple farming folk who rarely went ten miles from their home throughout their lives; but they were also shrewd and possessed of strong native intelligence

80 Old Labourer in Smock. A quite exceptional photograph by Gertrude Jekyll, author of *Old West Surrey* (Longmans, Green 1904)

81 Another of Miss Jekyll's photographs emphasizing the double bond, human to human and humans to the land beyond them

82 Labourers in white corduroy (c. 1900). It's the young now who wear corduroy suits and jackets

83 Old Bricklayer, West Surrey. He was stone deaf, left-handed and had lost one eye. 'But', writes Gertrude Jekyll, 'his work was some of the truest and best I have ever seen. His whole heart was in it.'

84 The Blacksmith at the turn of the century wore a short jacket of white baize or felt, a neat paper cap and a leather apron, the last being the most essential

85 Cottagers and their pot plants, a constant feature outside late Victorian labourers' cottages

86 Cider press in West Surrey. The heavy presser is screwed down on to the bags of pulp made from third grade apples, every ounce of juice for making the cider having been extracted

87 Cutting corn at Selsdon, 1902. These fields have now all been built over

88 Broom Squire's Cottage in the Devil's Punchbowl, at Hindhead, in 1907. This is the great glen nearly 900 feet below the highest point, where the granite cross put up by Lord Chief Justice Earle in 1851 stands next to the stone that marks the spot where the three murderers were hung in 1776

89 Ramming in dynamite to clear the site for making St George's Hill Golf Course near Weybridge. Seven thousand roots were blown up in this way

90 Shere, with charcoal burners, 1889. City livery companies cooked their great banquets on charcoal. The men providing the heat were also called 'colliers', a term which later included all miners

91 Family of gipsies on Mitcham Common 1881, a rather remarkable photograph by F C L Wratten

92 Ardbrook Common, family of gipsies, 1904

93 (*overleaf*) Sutton Park, 1900: woodmen

94 The cap was almost invariable indoor headgear; the heath broom was locally made and, at the turn of the century, cost 12½p per dozen!

COUNTRY TOWNS

95   Middle Row, from King Street, Croydon, c. 1890

96 Middle Row, Croydon, in 1890, recalling perhaps an Elizabethan description: 'deep hollow ways, and very dirty. The hotel on the right was unlikely to be noticed by the Egon Ronay of those days!

97 Market Field, Redhill in 1885

98 The Boathouse at Wandle Park, Croydon. The River Wandle itself rises in a garden at the southern end of Croydon, near Haling

99 Brighton Road, Croydon, south of the Swan and Sugar Loaf. The gig-drivers drove along the tramrails to avoid the potholes in the unmade road

100 North End, Croydon. The *Swan Inn*, next to the Whitgift Hospital, was pulled down in 1889. The Elizabethan hospital cost the Archbishop after whom it was named £2,700. From the original endowment grew the famous grammar school of the same name

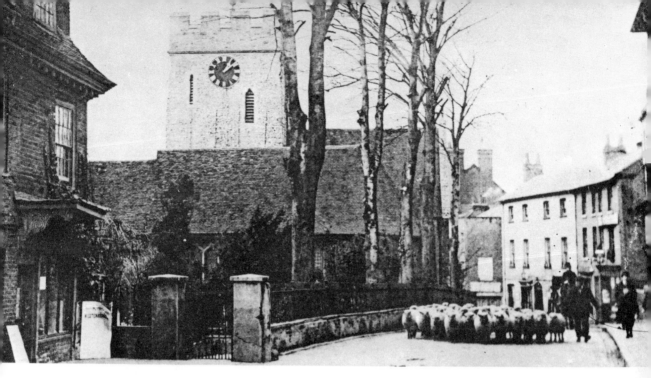

101 Guildford: St Mary's Church, with sheep being brought from the market through Quarry Street. This is the oldest Church in Guildford, in fact the oldest building in the town

102 The Old Smithy, Guildford High Street, which was pulled down in 1915

103   The Old Guildford Cattle Market in North Street. In 1895 the market was transferred to Woodbridge Road

104 The Old Boarden Bridge at Godalming (c. 1906). One of Surrey's most important rivers, the Wey, winds round the town

105 Godalming High Street, 1895. The town itself is dominated by the spires of Charterhouse School, which moved there from Smithfield in 1872

106 South Street, Dorking, in 1906, which even today retains some of the air of a market town

107 High Street Dorking at the turn of the century, a street justly famous throughout Surrey – and beyond

108 Dorking High Street, 1895, with the celebrated *White Horse Hotel* on the right. This inn was formerly known as the 'Cross House', it then being rented from the Knights of St John of Jerusalem at Clerkenwell. Some parts of the building are more than 400 years old

109 Epsom High Street, 1896. A quick glance in the dawn hours would suggest little change. But, although the clock tower and the steps on the right and one or two of the buildings remain, most of the rural character has gone

110   Garlands Road, Redhill, 1905. In *The Handbook to the Environs of London* (1876, reprinted 1970 by Adams & Dart) we learn that, following the arrival of a first class railway station, Redhill was 'marked as a quarry by the speculative builder, and on the hill-top has grown up a populous railway town of hideous brick shops and habitations.'

111   Looking down on Redhill, 1886, from the Pleasure Green

112   West Street Reigate (1906)

113   Reigate: Bell Street, adjoining the Priory, founded 700 years ago; and rebuilt in the eighteenth century as a great house. It is now a school and its grounds a public park

114   The Woodhatch Toll Gate, Reigate

115   The Old Post Office in the High Street of
Reigate, c. 1890

116   (*overleaf*) Reigate, 1891, with the 'excel-
lent family hotel', the *White Hart*, on the left.
In coaching days this was an important post on
the way to Brighton

117 Haslemere High Street, 1898, where Dr Jonathan Hutchinson established his extraordinary natural history museum

118 June 8th 1901, members of the SE Union of Scientific Societies meeting at Tennyson's house, Aldworth, near Haslemere, nine years after the poet's death

119 Purley Corner, 1903 The district once belonged to the Pirelea family, descending via Reginald de Pirle (1332) to John de Purle

120 Croydon Road, Caterham, 1891, a dull-looking village then as now, but within a mile of some of the most beautiful scenery in the country

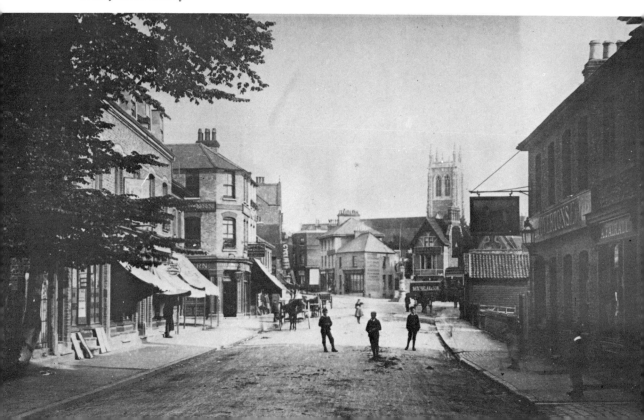

121 The last Esher Fair, 1880, with the Portsmouth Road as yet unmetalled. Now it is the scene of continuous thundering traffic

122 Reducing the level of the gradient of Lammas Lane, Esher in 1910–12

123 Croydon Road, Warlingham, 1907. Not long before this shot was taken it was described as 'a few humble cottages gathered about a broad Green, two or three sleepy shops, a smithy, a Methodist Chapel and a couple of little Inns.' Now it is just an extension of London

124 The Forge, Farleigh Road, Warlingham, 1905

125   The Rose and Crown Tea Gardens at Riddledown, near Caterham, 1907. A fossil fish's head was discovered here during the nineteenth century, leading to the belief that these great beds of chalk were once the bottom of an inland sea

126   Cobham Street, 1903. From the carriage outside the Post Office and Village Stores to the children safely standing across the road all is rural and peaceful and substantial – unbelievably only 17 miles from London

127 *The Jolly Farmer,* Farnham, 1903. William Cobbett was born in this inn in 1762. He is buried by the porch of the Norman chapel attached to the castle

PUBLIC LIFE AND OCCASIONS

128   Suffragette Week in Croydon 1909

129 Announcement of the Election results on the steps of the *Red Lion Hotel* (formerly 'The Cardinal's Cap'), Dorking. In the carriage on the left Mrs Hylton-Foster is talking to a policeman. The nanny beside her cradles a future Speaker of the House of Commons, Sir Harry Hylton-Foster

130 The Committee Room of the Unionists, Bletchingley, at the 1910 Election. Lord Palmerston once represented this village, though it was later disenfranchised

131   The Hampshire Yeomanry in Katherine Street, Croydon on May 19th 1896

132   Esher, June 23rd 1898. Inauguration of a new steamer by HRH The Princess Alice of Albany with the Duchess of Albany behind her

133 Crimean veteran's funeral at Addiscombe (c. 1905)

134   Figures and horses' heads for the Quadriga at Hyde Park Corner leave the foundry in Thames Ditton in 1912

SPORT AND ENTERTAINMENT

135 Coaches on the hill at the Epsom Race Course. The Earl of Derby founded
his famous race here towards the end of the eighteenth century. The 12th Earl
lived at The Oaks in nearby Woodmansterne, calling the great races after
himself and his house

137 The Surrey XI, 1883; C E Horner, Barrett, Pooley, Chester, W W Read, W E Roller, S W Cattley, Abel, J Shuter, Read, J M Henderson. In this year Surrey came fourth in the County Table, winning seven of their 16 matches

136 (*overleaf*) The Royal Box and Club Lawns at Sandown Park for the Eclipse Stakes Day. The racecourse is on the site of a small hospital founded in Norman times in Esher

138 Cricket Match at Norbury Hall, 1888, with G I Thornton's XI facing the Australians, and W G Grace batting. Thornton's XI made 144 and 63; the Australians 133 and 76 for 4

139 Kennington Cricket Ground, c. 1860, before the Oval was built

140 Golf on Reigate Heath, c. 1900

141 Golf at the Hindhead Golf Club in 1907, wonderful views all round (the highest point in Hindhead is over 900 feet above sea level)

142 The Wimbledon London Tennis Club in 1907, when it was still in Worple Road

143 Maids serving refreshments to the Surrey Union Hunt at Old Dene, near Dorking, in March 1912

144 Rifle competition between England and Scotland in 1898 at Bisley Camp, Brookwood near Woking. Brookwood also boasts the largest cemetery in England

145 Riflemen at the National Rifle Association's Range at Wimbledon c. 1889

146 Riflemen and spectators at the National Rifle Range, Wimbledon, c. 1889, looking much more like actors in an Indian period piece!

147 A Napier competing in the Byfleet Place at Brooklands on July 6th 1907

148 Ballooning at Ranelagh, May 1907. The destination of the race, announced just before the start, was Goring-on-Thames. The winner 'descended within a hundred yards of the stake'

149 Madame Florence, the Lady Globe Walker, as she passed through Redhill at 8.30 a.m. on Thursday July 18th 1903 on her journey from London to Brighton

150 Mr James Wellbelove and his colleagues from the Claygate Brickworks, c. 1898, no doubt *the* pop group of those days!

151 A Works Outing, taken outside the *Barley Mow,* Betchworth, probably on August Bank Holiday, 1900. The men came from William Johnson Ltd of Wandsworth Common, and the brake from Smith & Sons' livery stables at Tooting

152   A Punch and Judy Show at Croydon, 1905

153   Children (mainly) listening to a Hurdy Gurdy in Weimar Street, off the Lower Richmond Road, 1881

CHURCH, SCHOOL, ETC.

155 Five earnest clerics of Croydon, backing a printed postcard, whose legend includes the statement: a half-penny stamp for inland. One penny foreign. Both, of course, very pre-decimal

156   A group of boys and masters outside Castle School, Guildford, 1865

157   Esher Girls School, *c.* 1893: Class IV (with some of their younger sisters)

158   Wallington County School in 1905

SURREY EDUCATION COMMITTEE.

WALLINGTON COUNTY SCHOOL.   E S.A. LONDON. *Copyright.*

Never Absent, Never Late   *Leslie Bullett* 13.1.05

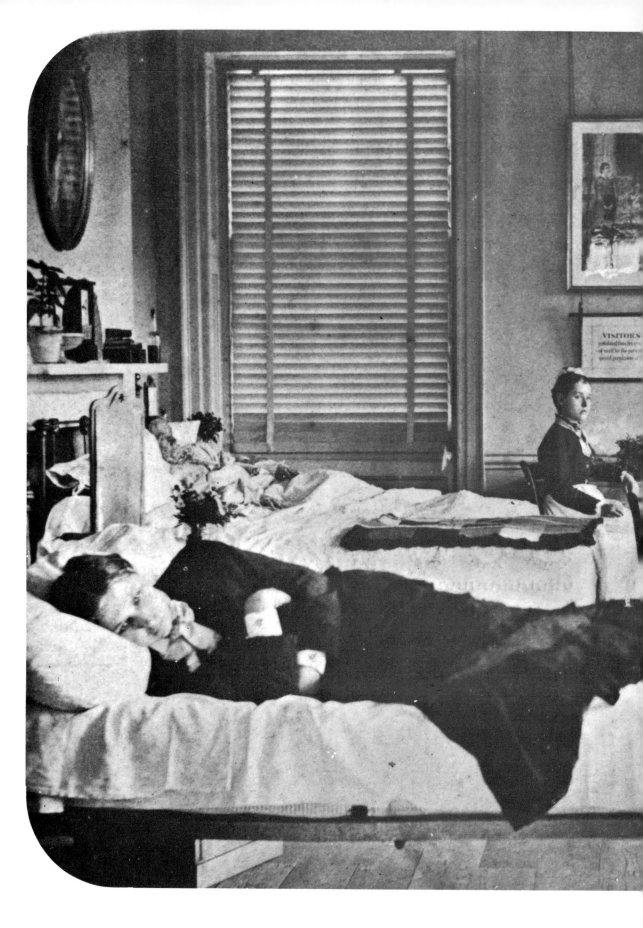

159 Duppas Hill Infirmary, Croydon

160   The first Croydon telephone exchange at 6 George Street, c. 1887

161 Erection of new chimney at the Weybridge Electricity Works, August 28th 1906

162 Laying the distributors in Ellesmere Road, Weybridge, c. 1906

163 (*overleaf*) The Guildford volunteers, who formed part of the 2nd Surrey Militia between 1870 and 1881

164   R F A Gun Drill at Deepcut Camp in 1905

165 The Gymnasium at Blackdown Camp in 1905

166   The miniature range at the Guards' Depot, Caterham (postmarked 1905)

167   Garrison Institute, Blackdown Camp, 1905